UNCOVERING AMERICAN HISTORY™

A PRIMARY SOURCE INVESTIGATION OF THE TRANSCONTINENTAL RAILROAD

Xina M. Uhl and Gillian Houghton

rosen publishing's rosen central®

New York

Published in 2019 by The Rosen Publishing Group, Inc.
29 East 21st Street, New York, NY 10010

First Edition

Cataloging-in-Publication Data

Names: Uhl, Xina M., author. | Houghton, Gillian, author.
Title: A primary source investigation of the Transcontinental Railroad / Xina M. Uhl and Gillian Houghton.
Description: New York : Rosen Publishing, 2019. | Series: Uncovering American history | Audience: Grades 5–8. | Includes bibliographical references and index.
Identifiers: ISBN 9781508184249 (library bound) | ISBN 9781508184232 (pbk.)
Subjects: LCSH: Union Pacific Railroad Company—History—Juvenile literature. | Central Pacific Railroad Company—History—Juvenile literature. | Railroads—United States—History—Juvenile literature.
Classification: LCC TF25.U5 U45 2019 | DDC 385.0973—dc23

Manufactured in the United States of America

On the cover: The painting shows A. J. Russell photographing the completion of the transcontinental railroad on May 10, 1869, in Promontory, Utah.

CONTENTS

INTRODUCTION

The story of the building of the United States's first transcontinental railroad is a uniquely American one. This railroad was spawned out of a relentless desire to conquer the landmass from the East Coast to the West Coast. Journalist John L. O'Sullivan wrote an 1845 article that clearly explained this impatient drive. Expansion, O'Sullivan argued, was "the right of our manifest destiny to overspread and to possess the whole of the continent which Providence has given us for the development of the great experiment of liberty and ... self-government entrusted to us." The term he used—manifest destiny—took root, and it described the driving factor that propelled lawmakers and laymen alike to support wars and treaties to widen the United States's size.

But once the western territory had been acquired, it needed to be adapted to the needs of the nation. Namely, the current slow, dangerous, costly methods of crossing the West made it extremely difficult to populate and to harvest its resources, like minerals and timber. The growing use and efficiency of railroads made them the best candidate for bridging the gap between the Pacific and Atlantic Oceans.

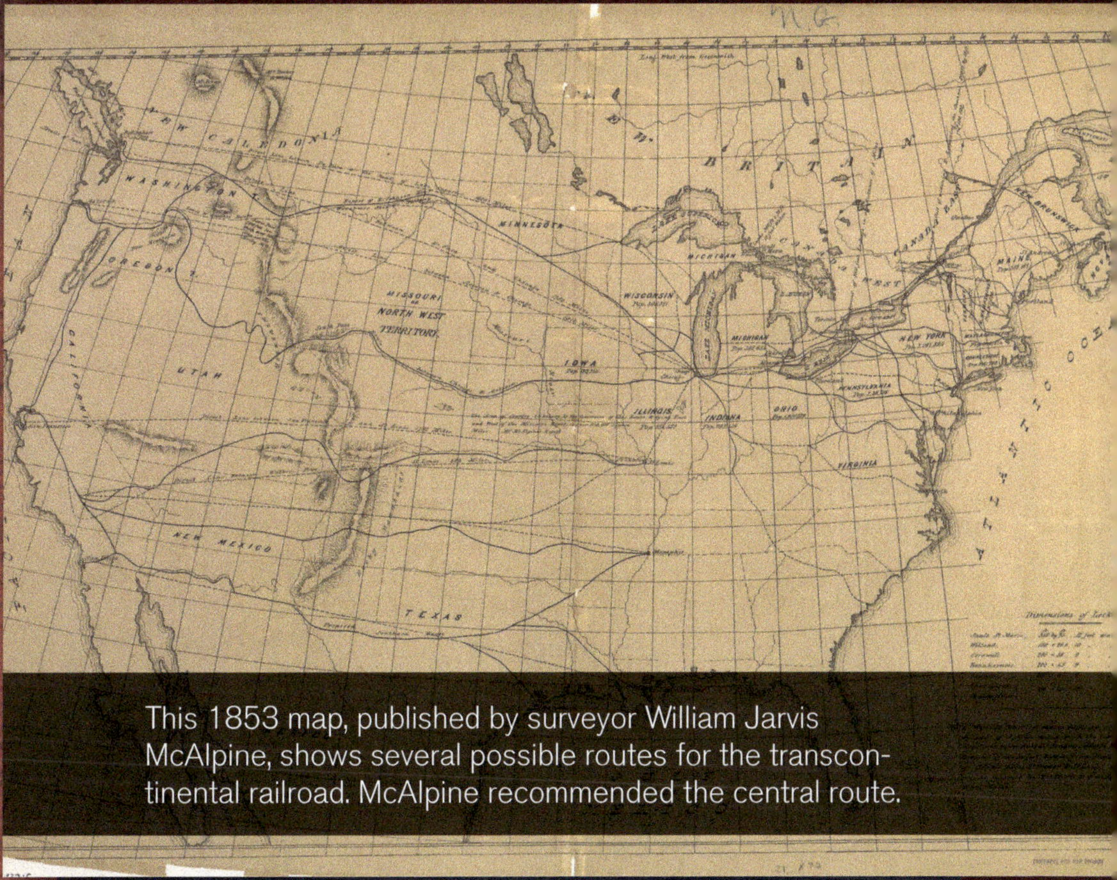

This 1853 map, published by surveyor William Jarvis McAlpine, shows several possible routes for the transcontinental railroad. McAlpine recommended the central route.

The story of the building of the transcontinental railroad has all the hallmarks of great drama: danger, greed, hardship, conflict, and an unstoppable drive to reach a goal. The people that came together to brave the wilderness and lay railroad ties across mountains and through what was known as the

Great American Desert included wily businessmen, impatient white settlers, proud Native Americans, hardworking Chinese immigrants, and a mix of recent Swedish and Irish immigrants.

In the midst of their hurry and hard labor, those who completed the railroad were aware of the great change it would bring to the nation. As reported in historian and author Stephen Ambrose's book *Nothing Like It in the World: The Men Who Built the Transcontinental Railroad*, Arthur Ferguson, a surveyor for the Union Pacific Railroad Company, made this observation as the railroad began its third year of construction in 1867: "The time is coming and fast too, when in the sense it is now understood, there will be no west." Ferguson was correct in many ways.

The transcontinental railroad's completion meant that continent-wide travel and communication were now possible. The widely scattered and isolated settlements west of the Mississippi River would become connected. Scientific happenings, cultural events, and political events and notions could be reported instantaneously over telegraph wires, which were erected beside the track bed as the rails were laid. Products like cattle could be carried by rail to a national marketplace with increasing speed and efficiency. The railroad would spur the growth of a new type of business—corporations—which not only made the creation of a national stock exchange possible, but also drove the business powerhouses to come.

CHAPTER ONE

GOING WEST

The legacy of the railroad is greater than just an increase in marketplaces and business wealth. It is a legacy of new cities that began as railroad camps, of plains wiped clear of the endless herds of American buffalo, of the near-destruction of Native American tribes like the Sioux and Cheyenne, and, ultimately, of modern America.

The 1840s saw a great widening of the United States's borders. When Congress annexed Texas in 1845, a war with Mexico followed. The United States won that war, and Mexico handed over a huge swath of land: California, Nevada, Arizona, and parts of Wyoming, Colorado, Utah, and New Mexico. An agreement with Britain in 1846 allowed the United States to absorb the Oregon Territory, today's states of Washington and Oregon. This land held mystery since most of it was inhabited only by Native Americans.

GOLD FEVER

Then, in 1848, a phenomenal lode of gold was discovered about 40 miles (64 kilometers) west of

Sacramento, California. The promise of riches hidden in the foothills of the Sierra Nevada had come true; there was gold in the mountains. In only a few years, dozens of settlements dotted the West Coast. Young men from the East risked their savings and their lives to test their luck in the California wilderness. In 1850 alone, fifty-five thousand men began the journey to California. By 1860, more than three hundred thousand men (and a small group of women) had traveled west with dreams of striking it rich.

There were three ways to get from New York and other industrialized cities in the East to the booming gold mining towns of California and Nevada. A traveler could take the train to Omaha, Nebraska, and then board a stagecoach bound for the treacherous mountain paths of the Rocky Mountains and Sierra Nevada. If wild animals or bands of Sioux or Cheyenne didn't raid the coach along the way, a traveler might arrive safely at his or her destination.

A second alternative was to sail around Cape Horn, the southern tip of South America, on a crowded, expensive schooner. After arriving in San Francisco or Sacramento, the traveler would take a wagon or stagecoach to his or her destination. A final option was to travel by ship to the Isthmus of Panama in Central America, travel on foot or by coach over land, and sail from the western coast of Panama to California. In fair weather, the trip over land through the United States could take more than six months. Ships bound for Cape Horn were often robbed by pirates and burned at sea. Travelers across the Isthmus of Panama nearly always got sick.

Broadsides like W. R. Andrews's were printed in newspapers and distributed in towns. People were anxious for as much information about the vast western wilderness as possible. Andrews promised details of "the bays, rivers, navigation, trade, mines, minerals, animals, vegetable productions . . . Indians, &c. manner of digging and washing gold, amount procured by different individuals and many other interesting facts relative to California." In other words, Andrews claimed to offer everything an adventurer would need to know to get started.

Because the trip to California by stagecoach or boat was very difficult, people soon looked to the railroads to provide safe, fast overland travel. The first steam-powered boats navigated the Mississippi River in 1807, but it wasn't until nearly two decades later that the technology involved in harnessing steam power was applied to the locomotive.

This lantern slide from the 1870s shows the paddle steamer *Lake Superior*, owned by the Northern Line Packet Company, which operated riverboat services on the Mississippi River.

RAILROADS COME

These early trains were dirty, dangerous, and slow. They belched out thick columns of smoke that drifted downwind of the tracks. Passengers spent the bumpy ride perched uncomfortably on uneven, backless benches. Each car had a separate brake, which had to be pulled by hand, making emergency or unexpected stops impossible. Discomfort aside, to the traveler of the mid-nineteenth century, these trains were powerful iron horses (as new trains came to be called). It became clear to railroad investors, the government, and the public at large that the best way to exploit the natural resources of the West and protect the new settlements of the frontier was to build an iron road that connected the East and West. The railroads could carry lumber and other raw materials to the factories in the East and transport army troops from their homes in the East to the isolated forts in the West.

Major General Grenville M. Dodge of the Union army, shown here, built railroads during the Civil War.

The prospect of a coast-to-coast railroad was met with much enthusiasm. Newspaper editorials and railroad journals applauded the idea, politicians demanded it, and a few enterprising surveyors went into the wilderness to look for the best route for the railroad to follow. This was a courageous feat. Surveyors had to learn the ins and outs of thousands of square miles of land inhabited by Indians and wild animals. Their equipment was often limited to a compass, a level, and a pack mule.

In 1853, Congress authorized government-sponsored explorations—known as the Pacific Railroad Surveys—under the supervision of Secretary of War Jefferson Davis. Five possible routes were determined, and the surveyors presented their reports to Congress in twelve volumes. The northern route followed the forty-seventh latitude from St. Paul, Minnesota, to Seattle, in the Washington Territory. The central route ran along the Platte River Valley, from Omaha, Nebraska, to San Francisco, California. A third route, called the Buffalo Trail, ran through the Colorado Territory. Two southern routes ran through the New Mexico and Arizona Territories to southern California. Eventually, trains would travel each of these paths, and modern engineers would make few improvements on the original routes. In 1853, however, political, economic, and social divisions between the southern and northern states prevented Congress from choosing a route. Even as Congress sat stalled during the following decade, surveyors headed west. One such surveyor was Grenville Dodge.

Grenville Dodge was born in Massachusetts on April 12, 1831. He began working for the railroad at the age of fourteen. After studying engineering at Norwich University in Vermont, he moved to Illinois, where the railroad revolution was beginning. Dodge was eager and strong-willed, and he had ambitious plans for the future of the railways. In 1856, funded by Wall Street businessman Thomas Durant and railroad investor Henry Farnam, Dodge led an expedition to survey the Platte Valley route.

The land west of the Missouri River was a great expanse of flat, dusty plains, rolling hills, river valleys, and sheltering woods leading to the foothills of the Rocky Mountains. Long before Dodge began his surveys, each year the Cheyenne and Sioux had followed the buffalo

AN UNLIKELY FRIEND TO RAILROADS

Abraham Lincoln was a long-standing proponent of the railroad industry. During his terms as an Illinois state representative (1834–1842) and congressman (1847–1849), the Illinois Central Railroad grew steadily, soon exceeding in length any other railroad network in the world. In his campaign for the Republican nomination for the presidency of the United States, Lincoln advocated a railroad from coast to coast. The primary obstacle facing the construction of a transcontinental railroad was the issue of slavery. Secretary of War Jefferson Davis, who would go on to be the president of the Confederacy during the Civil War, argued for the southern route from New Orleans, Louisiana, to San Diego, California. This route would extend slavery by connecting southern slave states and the uncharted, unregulated western frontier. No free state would agree to the southern route. Likewise, the northerners wanted the railroad to begin in Chicago or St. Paul, but no southern politician would accept this.

herds along the Platte Valley route. The same path was taken by the Rocky Mountain fur-trading companies and, after them, by a group of religious exiles from the East and Midwest known as the Mormons, who were on their way to a new settlement in the wilderness of Utah. The route was ideal for travel by foot or by rail; the river provided a source of freshwater, and the flat land was easy to navigate in a straight, level line.

When Dodge completed his initial surveys, he traveled to New York City to meet with the directors of Durant's investment company and to present his plans for a railroad along the Platte River. By the end of the meeting, the only people left in the room were Grenville Dodge, Thomas Durant, and Henry Farnam; the other businessmen had left in disbelief. The three remaining men were the only ones who believed the project could be done.

THE REPUBLICAN PARTY

At the 1860 Republican National Convention, delegates adopted one of the most important party platforms in American history. In it, the Republican Party described the slave trade as "a crime against humanity and a burning shame to our country and age." The party pledged to "call upon Congress to take prompt and efficient measures for the total and final suppression" of slavery in the United States. The following fall, Lincoln was elected president, in part on the strength of his antislavery message. To defend the institution of slavery and their sovereignty, thirteen southern states seceded from the Union. On April 12, 1861, the first shots of the American Civil War were fired at Fort Sumter in South Carolina.

The 1860 Republican platform also said that "a Railroad to the Pacific Ocean is imperatively demanded by the interests of the whole country" and that Congress should offer immediate aid for its construction. Instead of dampening America's enthusiasm for the railroads, the outbreak of war solved the problem of determining the iron horse's route. The Union Congress, now made up of only free-state politicians, faced no opposition in choosing a northern route. They immediately began debating and drafting a bill to organize and finance the construction of a transcontinental railroad along the Platte Valley route. On July 1, 1862, Lincoln signed the Pacific Railroad Act.

NATIONAL REPUBLICAN
PLATFORM
ADOPTED BY THE
NATIONAL REPUBLICAN CONVENTION,
HELD IN CHICAGO, MAY 17, 1860.

The National Republican Convention was held in Chicago on May 17, 1860. See transcription on pages 50–54.

The Pacific Railroad Act provided financial incentives to corporations that undertook the construction of the railroad. Two corporations would rise to the task. The Central Pacific Railroad would build east from Sacramento, California, and the Union Pacific Railroad would build west from Omaha, Nebraska. They would meet at a town to be determined by Congress at a later date. The government would allot a certain number of acres of land on either side of the railroad for every mile of track that was laid. The railroad companies would build stations and warehouses on this valuable land or sell it to settlers to offset construction costs.

For each mile of track laid, the government would also give each railroad company a certain number of government bonds, which could also be sold for each company's profit. However, as Dodge discovered in his 1856 meeting with Durant and Farnam, many investors would be wary of the proposition. Building a railroad from coast to coast was a job for a remarkable man, one who was part engineer, part accountant, part wise man, part politician, and part swindler.

It would take not one but five men to rise to the challenge. The men of the Central Pacific Railroad Company were risk takers and adventurers who dreamed of being part of something monumental.

CHAPTER TWO

FOUR TYCOONS

In 1849, gold miners—called forty-niners—flooded into California to strike it rich. Few succeeded in that goal. But along with them came four men who would become titans of industry. They headed the Central Pacific Railroad, and their names were Leland Stanford, Collis P. Huntington, Charles Crocker, and Mark Hopkins.

THEODORE JUDAH

But it was a young Connecticut engineer named Theodore Judah who would offer these four men the business opportunity that would make them California legends. Judah was an experienced surveyor and engineer from the East Coast. In 1854, he moved his family from New York to Sacramento, California, to work on the first railroad west of the Mississippi River. The line ran from Sacramento to Folsom, California, just west of the Sierra Nevada, and it served the gold miners of Placerville, California.

Upon the railroad's completion in 1855, Judah dreamed of building something even bigger—a train line from coast to coast. Judah believed that a railroad of such size and expense would have to be sponsored by the government. While employed as chief engineer of the Sacramento Valley and the Sacramento Valley Central Railroads, Judah traveled to Washington, D.C., to promote a coast-to-coast railroad.

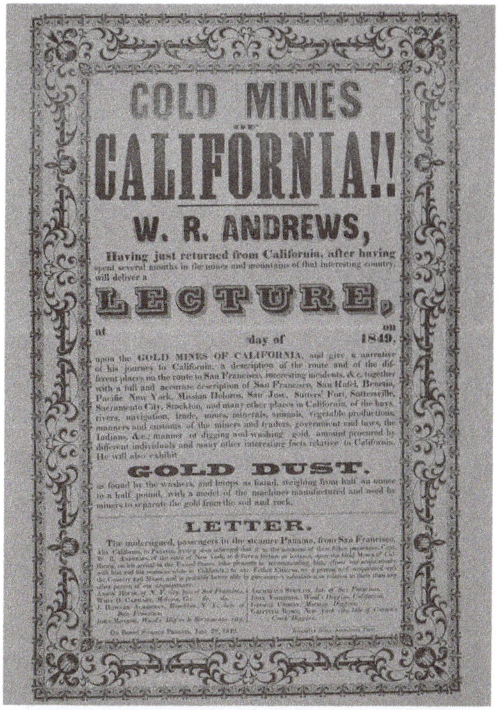

This 1849 ad appeared in the *Rochester Daily Advertiser*. The letter at the bottom endorsed the speaker's qualifications.

At his own expense, he published a promotional pamphlet that he distributed to every member of Congress, and he pitched his idea to anyone who would listen. Congress was deadlocked, or unable to make a decision by a majority; disagreements between free and slave states defeated all of Judah's endeavors in Washington. Disheartened, he returned to Sacramento. In 1859, a convention of local politicians and businessmen organized by the California legislature decided that the western terminus, or end, of the transcontinental railroad should be Sacramento, California. Judah was chosen by the group to relay the decision to Washington and to continue his efforts there at the expense of these local investors.

A MINIMUSEUM

In 1859, Theodore Judah set up an office in Washington's Capitol that served as a mini-museum of his plans for a transcontinental railroad. Unlike Jefferson Davis's 1853 surveys, Judah's exhibits detailed the exact path of the line, how many cubic feet of earth would have to be moved to keep a level or gentle incline, and other specifics of laying track. Maps and mineral samples were carefully displayed. His surveys considered other factors, such as snow and foul weather, population, and the construction of locomotives. However, Judah's exhibits failed to explain how the railroad would cross the wide rivers, the Great Basin of Nevada, and, most important, the Sierra Nevada.

In the summer of 1860, Judah returned to California in order to perform a detailed survey of the Sierra Nevada, to determine the line of the railroad track through this phenomenal mountain range, and to form the corporation that would build the railroad.

After countless cold nights sleeping on the ground, cooking meals over an open fire, hiking hundreds of miles, and scaling treacherous mountain passes in search of a route, the task was accomplished. At the suggestion of a pharmacist from Dutch Flat, California, named Daniel W. Strong, Judah surveyed Donner Pass and determined that it was the best route through the mountains for the railroad.

FOUNDING OF THE CENTRAL PACIFIC

At Dr. Strong's store in Dutch Flat, Judah drew up the Articles of Association. It served as a preliminary outline of the organization of the company that would later become the Central Pacific Railroad. A month and a half later, Lincoln was elected president, and the dream of a railroad to Sacramento became a real possibility.

When Judah returned to Sacramento in November 1860, he held a series of open meetings at the St. Joseph Hotel. There, he presented his plan for a railroad spanning to the Sierra Nevada (and perhaps as far as the state line of Nevada) to a crowd of businessmen. His real goal was a coast-to-coast railroad, but in his presentation to potential investors, Judah scaled back his plans to avoid appearing fanatical or crazy.

Leland Stanford was both a lawyer and a shopkeeper who moved to California in 1852 and entered state politics.

Leland Stanford and three other Sacramento businessmen, Collis P. Huntington, Charles Crocker, and Mark Hopkins, were among the crowd at the St. Joseph one night and at a smaller meeting soon after, and they liked the idea. The railroad would connect their stores with the markets of the Nevada mining towns, and if they owned the railroad, they would set the price of transporting their goods. If a railroad over the mountains proved financially impossible, Judah argued, he would build the merchants a wagon road (a flat roadbed) east from Dutch Flat, from which they could expect huge profits by charging high tolls. The four men invested private money to fund a more complete survey of the route. Judah left for the mountains in the spring of 1861 to conduct this final survey.

STANFORD

On June 28, 1861, the Central Pacific Railroad was officially created, and Leland Stanford, who was about to be elected governor of California, was chosen as president of the company. Stanford would go on to become the third president of the Southern Pacific Company, the founder of Stanford University in Palo Alto, California, and the most famous of the Big Four, as the Sacramento store owners came to be called. He became an important figure in local and national government and was a close friend of Abraham Lincoln's. He had a reputation as a fair, friendly man who was often called upon to settle disputes between local miners and businessmen.

However, first and foremost, the Big Four were businessmen. They expected a profit from their investment in the Central Pacific, and they would do almost anything to achieve this goal. Though the public came to trust and admire the powerful California railroad moguls, in truth, they were corrupt businessmen and ruthless bosses.

As president of the company, Stanford's job was to court public opinion and use his political influence to raise money from county and state government agencies. By

1863, Stanford had secured millions of dollars from the state of California. The Central Pacific would transport convicts, members of the state militia, and materials for agricultural fairs for free. In return, the railroad would receive state bonds that could be sold for the company's profit. This was an important deal. Many people demanded the construction of the railroad, but few were brave enough to invest in it. The general opinion was that the four Sacramento store owners were going to lose their fortunes and their reputations as businessmen in the wild peaks and deep gorges of the Sierra Nevada.

HUNTINGTON

Collis P. Huntington headed to California in 1849 and made a fortune selling mining equipment to gold seekers.

Collis P. Huntington was chosen as vice president of the Central Pacific Railroad. From his office in New York City (he had moved there after the formation of the Central Pacific, but he still owned the store in California), he sold stock and bought construction materials, including iron rails, shovels, picks, and wooden ties, which would then be shipped around Cape Horn to the end of the track. Once the construction of the railroad was under way, supplying the crews with materials to lay the track became a full-time job. Ships filled with materials were often lost at sea. During the Civil War, the price of raw materials, such as black powder and iron, skyrocketed.

Huntington also traveled throughout the Northeast to pitch his new business to potential investors, but no one would take a chance on the struggling railroad. If completed, potential investors argued, the railroad might not see a profit for more than twenty years. In addition, the Civil War had destabilized the American economy. Paper money was often worth as little as thirty-five cents on the dollar. Huntington was forced to offer banks and investors Central Pacific bonds to secure loans. As well, he used his own investment in the company, his reputation as a businessman, and government aid that the company had not yet earned as collateral for private loans.

CROCKER

As a member of the board of directors for the Central Pacific, Charles Crocker established a construction contracting business called the Charles Crocker Contract and Finance Company. He then awarded his firm the job of contracting the construction of the first stretch of railroad from Sacramento to Roseville, California. Crocker's firm was responsible for hiring construction companies to build the railroad, its stations, and its warehouses and for supplying these construction companies with all of the materials and building equipment they required. In return, the Central Pacific would pay Crocker $400,000 in cash and Central Pacific stock for the first 18 miles (29 km) of track.

The Big Four were the only stockholders in Crocker Contract and Finance. Therefore, the cash and Central Pacific stock that Crocker's firm was paid for the job was divided among them. Whatever money came into the

Central Pacific coffers—from the government or from private investors—was circulated within the Big Four. Crocker's scheme was so complicated that the extent of the scam remains unclear even today. Judah was not a stockholder in Crocker Contract and Finance, and he began to fear that the Big Four, in an effort to make a profit from the railroad's construction, would drive it into bankruptcy.

HOPKINS

In 1861, Mark Hopkins was chosen as the treasurer of the Central Pacific Railroad. He was the eldest of the Big Four and was considered the wisest of the group. Eventually, all decisions had to be approved by Hopkins. As it turned out, the construction of the Central Pacific was more complicated than anyone had anticipated. Public opinion had turned against the Big Four. Critics accused the Central Pacific of using the government funds allotted to the company by the Pacific Railroad Act to lay tracks only as far as Dutch Flat. From there, travelers would have to follow the Big Four's toll road to the Nevada mines.

Most significantly, tensions were mounting within the company. One important debate between Judah and the Big Four was over where the Sierra Nevada officially began. The Central Pacific was given more government funds for track laid over the mountain range and its foothills than for track laid over flat land. The Big Four believed it was in the company's immediate financial interest to extend the official limits of the mountain range as far west toward Sacramento as possible. Crocker arranged to have surveys taken to establish the foothills as beginning at Arcade Creek, 7 miles (11 km) east of the Sacramento River. Judah believed this obvious fabrication would not endear the company to lawmakers and potential investors, even though it would fund the railroad on a more immediate schedule. In addition, Judah was increasingly distrustful of the Crocker Contract and Finance scheme.

Judah and several other members of the board of directors were convinced that the Big Four had to be bought out. However, in the end, Judah could not raise the money to buy their stock and was compelled to sell his share in the company to the Big Four. Though he was still chief engineer, Judah no longer owned stock in the railroad. He made a final trip to New York to meet with investors he hoped would buy out the Big Four and save the Central Pacific from corruption and ruin. On the trip, he contracted yellow fever in Panama. He arrived in New York and died a week later, on November 2, 1863.

★ CHAPTER THREE

PICKAXES AND RAILROAD TIES

The first Pacific Railroad Act, which became law in 1862, affected the character and landscape of the United States like few other pieces of legislation had done. In order to complete the nation's first transcontinental railroad, it offered "men of talent, men of character, men who are willing to invest" incentives to complete the task. It specified that the work would be completed by two railroad firms—the Central Pacific, which would work from west to east, and the newly formed Union Pacific, which would work from east to west. The two tracks would meet somewhere in the middle.

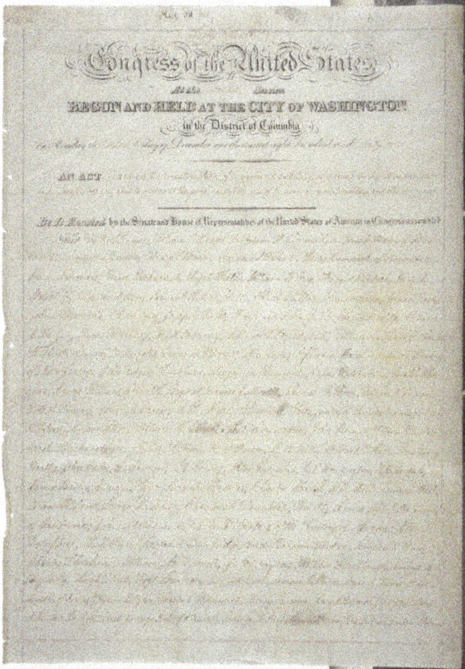
Congress of the United States
BEGUN AND HELD AT THE CITY OF WASHINGTON
in the District of Columbia
AN ACT
Be it enacted by the Senate and House of Representatives of the United States of America in Congress assembled

The 1862 Pacific Railway Act authorized construction of the transcontinental railroad. See transcription on pages 54–55.

CRÉDIT MOBILIER

Veteran railroad man General John A. Dix was the Union Pacific's first president, but he was eventually replaced by Oliver Ames, a shovel manufacturer from Boston. Throughout the construction of the railroad, Thomas Durant served as vice president and was the company's real leader. Like the Big Four, Durant was in the railroad business to make money, and he and George Train pioneered a great swindle in an attempt to secure a profit.

The two men bought an unsuccessful corporation based in Pennsylvania and renamed it Crédit Mobilier of America. They sold over $300,000 in stock in the company. The Union Pacific, under Durant's orders, awarded construction contracts to Crédit Mobilier and paid the company in cash. Crédit Mobilier, or rather Durant, used the money to buy Union Pacific stocks and bonds at face value and then sold them for an inflated price on the open market or used them as collateral to secure loans.

By selling the stocks, Crédit Mobilier could make a huge profit even if Union Pacific never laid a single rail. However, by rewarding its investors with huge annual dividends, Crédit Mobilier and the Union Pacific were always on the verge of bankruptcy.

THE UNION PACIFIC RAILROAD

The act provided for the formation of the Union Pacific Railroad Company, to be led by 163 commissioners. These men selected Samuel R. Curtis as their temporary chairman and agreed to begin selling stock in the company at once. They were able to sell sizable interests in the company to only three men. Brigham Young, the leader of the Mormons, bought the largest share, while both Thomas Durant, who had funded General Grenville Dodge's initial surveys, and George Francis Train invested in twenty shares each.

Like the Central Pacific, the Union Pacific begged and borrowed for money to build the railroad. Chief engineer Grenville Dodge was constantly suspicious of Durant's greed, and to protect Crédit Mobilier, Durant constantly questioned Dodge's authority. However, despite the disagreements between the company's vice president and its chief engineer, the Union Pacific built a railroad in record time.

THE WORK

The railroads employed thousands of men who broke through uncharted wilderness and laid timber and iron ties at the speed of a walking horse. On any given day, laborers were scattered on either side of a 200-mile (322 km)-long line. They built the railroad in waves, each crew performing a particular task with speed and precision. Using picks and shovels, men known as graders were the first crews to follow the line the surveyors had marked out with wooden spikes. The graders carved cuts, filled ravines, and cleared the roadbed of vegetation, rocks, and trees. Hundreds of thousands of cubic yards of earth were carried in or hauled out using an army of handcarts pushed by men or pulled by horses.

This movie still from the Cecil B. DeMille film *Union Pacific* depicted a construction scene from the building of the transcontinental railroad.

When they reached the mountains, the graders used black powder and nitroglycerin to blast through miles of rock and to carve tunnels out of solid granite and limestone. A path of earth 2 feet (61 centimeters) high and 12 feet (3.7 km) wide was scraped and padded down with heavy steel plows pulled by oxen or horses. The grade was packed by hand with stone ballast or sand. The next crew laid the ties—between 2,260 and 2,640 per mile of track. Then came the men who laid the rails.

Horse-drawn wagons traveled along the track, each carrying about forty rails and an appropriate number of spikes and chairs (pieces of iron that supported the rails on the track). The wagons would stop just before the end of the line, and five men would gather on either side. Then, two men would raise one end of a rail, and three men would seize the other end, guiding it as it slid out of the wagon. Each rail weighed about 700 pounds (317 kilograms). The chairs were put in place by another gang of men. When the foreman shouted "Down!" the men carrying the rails dropped them into place. A man known as the gauger would kneel down to check the distance between the two parallel rails. When instructed, the laborer known as the spiker would pound in a spike with a loud blow from his sledgehammer. Two parallel rails were laid every thirty seconds, and the mighty ring of the sledgehammer sounded like clockwork.

Not long after the sound of the sledgehammer faded, the company carpenters arrived. They built stations, warehouses, and offices on the land granted to the railroads by the government. Towns were laid out with care by railroad supervisors, and lots were sold at auction to newly arrived settlers.

The work crews were followed by a band of several thousand nomadic bartenders, gamblers, prostitutes, thieves, and confidence men (con men). Each night, they built temporary towns of tents and clapboard buildings in the open fields along the railroad or on the outskirts of the company towns. They catered to the rowdy railroad workers, mostly young men who were far from home and who had a steady income.

This color engraving from 1869 shows the railroad station in the new town of Laramie, Wyoming. The large water tank and windmill were used to fill up steam locomotives with water.

THE TOWNS AND THE TRACKS

The towns at the end of the track were known as hell-on-wheels towns. They averaged one murder per day, and their residents were universally criticized as a "congregation of scum" (as travel writer Samuel Bowles puts it in Stephen Ambrose's *Nothing Like It in the World*). Many hell-on-wheels towns, like Benton, Wyoming, disappeared after the railroad moved on, leaving behind only a small cemetery. Others, like Cheyenne, Wyoming, which General Grenville Dodge considered one of the worst places he had ever seen, survived and flourished. Wood-frame houses replaced the canvas tents, and honest business owners settled in the community. Slowly but surely, the railroads drew people west, and towns grew on the dusty, alkali plains of Wyoming.

Westward settlement flourished at the expense of North America's Indian populations. In 1862, Congress ratified the Homestead Act, which granted every US citizen the right to claim 160 acres (65 hectares) of land in the western frontier. The central plains, soon to be connected to both coasts by rail, were flooded with eager settlers. Towns grew, and farms cultivated the land where buffalo had once grazed, causing the buffalo herds to starve.

As the railroad stretched across the country, dividing it north from south, it also interrupted the seasonal migration of the buffalo, who would not cross the tracks. In addition, the railroad men found sport in shooting buffalo and leaving their carcasses to rot. By the end of the nineteenth century, the buffalo, which had been the foundation of the Indian economy for generations, were nearly eliminated. Plains Indians, including the Sioux and Cheyenne, attempted to defend their land and way of life from the whites and the railroad, which was a powerful symbol of white expansion. War parties attacked the railroad camps, stole horses and oxen, destroyed supplies, and killed laborers and train passengers. Telegraph poles were torn down, wooden track ties were removed or burned, rails were undone, and trains were run off the mangled tracks.

In response, the US government employed Pawnee warriors to defend the railroad camps and the growing

A group of Pawnee warriors poses in front of a Union Pacific passenger car in October 1866. The Pawnee had been invited to nearby Columbus, Nebraska, to entertain tourists.

white settlements from hostile tribes. The Sioux and Cheyenne referred to the Pawnee as "Hang Around the Forts," suggesting that they were willing pawns in the hands of whites. However, the Pawnee were longtime enemies of the Sioux and Cheyenne, and the Pawnee warriors enjoyed their work and the safety provided by the US government. The army supplied the Pawnee with food, clothing, money, and the newest Springfield rifles.

Nonetheless, even the US military was not equipped to protect the settlers or railroad laborers at every moment, so General Grenville Dodge insisted that every man working on the railroad be armed. When armed, the Union Pacific laborers—mostly well-trained Civil War veterans—were able to defend themselves. As a general in the army and chief engineer of the railroad, Dodge played a part in the destruction of the Plains nations. The Indian population quickly dwindled, and their traditional way of life came to an end. Ultimately, the Indians were forced to either live on government-organized reservations or risk death in the new West.

★ CHAPTER FOUR

THE SIERRA NEVADA AND BEYOND

The Central Pacific Railroad had one problem in particular. The young adventurers who had signed up to work in Sacramento left when the railroad made it to eastern California, where they hoped to strike it rich. No local population from which to hire lived in the isolated hills and canyons of the Sierra Nevada. In spring 1865, the Big Four needed five thousand men. They had only eight hundred. Charles Crocker suggested that they hire fifty local Chinese laborers.

THE CHINESE

Stephen Ambrose reports in N*othing Like It in the World* that when Crocker suggested hiring Chinese workers, James Harvey Strobridge, the Central Pacific's superintendent of construction, replied, "I will not boss Chinese!" The Chinese were considered weak and unmanly. Strobridge eventually relented but gave the Chinese the relatively simple task of filling horse-drawn carts with rubble. The Chinese were so hardworking in this and every subsequent task they were given that the Central Pacific came to depend on them for their most dangerous and labor-intensive jobs, while the skilled work of masonry, carpentry, and laying rail was reserved for white laborers.

The Chinese workers, usually led by Irish bosses, were hired to dig trenches and fill gaps, cut down trees, and carve out tunnels by hand. They were originally hired at $28 per month (about $304 today) but were soon paid $31 per month (about $336 today). Their sleeping quarters were provided for, but not their food. By the end of 1865, the Central Pacific employed more than seven thousand Chinese laborers and only two thousand white laborers.

EAGER IMMIGRANTS

The Chinese had come to California in the same flood of immigration that had brought Stanford, Crocker, and Hopkins to the West Coast. Nearly sixty thousand young Chinese men had dreams of striking it rich in the gold mines, but there were many obstacles in their way. They were bullied and often robbed when they approached the large mines; therefore, they worked primarily on smaller, less profitable mines. Unlike their white counterparts, they were forced to pay a miner's tax, a permission tax, and a water tax. They were

(continued on the next page)

(continued from the previous page)

also taxed for hospitals, property, and public schools, which they were not allowed to attend. They were not allowed to obtain citizenship or to testify in court. They were regularly robbed, beaten, or killed by their employers and rival miners. In 1858, the California legislature passed a law prohibiting their immigration, but they continued to come.

Chinese laborers working on the transcontinental railroad system pose for a photo in 1880. Most of these immigrants came from southern China.

DANGEROUS WORK

The army of Chinese laborers faced their most difficult task in the fall of 1866, when they began work on the Summit Tunnel. The Summit Tunnel was the sixth tunnel on the road from Sacramento. It cut through a peak of the Sierra Nevada 7,017 feet (2,139 meters) above sea level. The tunnel was 1,659 feet (506 m) long. Initially, the men attacked the granite wall from either side, but eventually, they cut a 90-foot (27 m)-long shaft down into the rock from the top. Laborers were lowered into the shaft in baskets and worked from the inside out in both directions while another crew of laborers worked from the outside in.

Narrow holes were made with hand drills. The laborers packed black powder into the holes, lit the fuses, and shouted a warning. The men on the outside would run as far away as possible, while the men in the shaft were quickly lifted out in baskets. Once the explosion was over and the smoke cleared, the men went back to pick away at the rock.

Four hundred men drilled away at the Summit Tunnel in eight- or nine-hour shifts twenty-four hours a day. Each day, they made less than a foot of progress on each face. As the winter of 1866 to 1867 approached, the snow accumulated in drifts of up to 30 feet (9 m). That year, there were forty-four storms in the Sierra Nevada peaks. The Chinese were forced to carve tunnels in the snow that led from their camps to the work site. Windows and chimneys were cut in the walls of snow to provide a glimpse of the sky. The workmen lived in a maze of tunnels under the snow for many months.

An untold number of men died in the construction of the Central Pacific. Many were caught in the black-powder explosions or buried alive under an avalanche of rock or

As the Central Pacific Railroad carved its way from Sacramento to Promontory Summit in Utah, it had to cut fifteen tunnels through solid granite—a feat that had never before been attempted.

snow. Sometimes, their bodies were found when the snow melted the following spring, their shovels and picks still tightly clutched in their hands. When winter set in, food and other supplies were not regularly delivered, and the laborers faced starvation. The wind howled, and the camp was bitterly cold. The men continued to pick away at the granite face for over a year, completing the tunnel and laying the rails by November 1867.

THE MORMONS

The dusty, inhospitable land that would later become the states of Nebraska and Wyoming were known as part of the Great American Desert. Summers were hot and dry while winters were bitterly cold. The railroad route drained the North Platte River of water. The rare trees were not the hardwoods necessary to make wooden rail ties. All of the materials had to be shipped by steamboat along the Missouri River and by rail from Omaha to the end of the track.

Just as the Union Pacific had crossed the desolate border between Nebraska and Wyoming, the Central Pacific penetrated the Summit Tunnel. According to the Pacific Railroad Act, the company that laid the most rail the fastest received the most money and the largest share of land grants. The directors of both companies were willing to go to any length to finish first, but they were just as likely to cut corners to save time and money. Consequently, parts of the railroad were poorly constructed or simply left unfinished. The track, laid on an uneven and unstable grade, curved sharply and climbed steep inclines. The wooden bridges and snowsheds were fire hazards. The ties were made of a brittle wood that would need to be replaced in three years' time.

The Union Pacific sped through Wyoming, laying up to 4 miles (6 km) of track in a single day. They made it well into Utah by the end of 1868. On January 9, 1869, the Union Pacific had laid 1,000 miles (1,609 km) of track west of

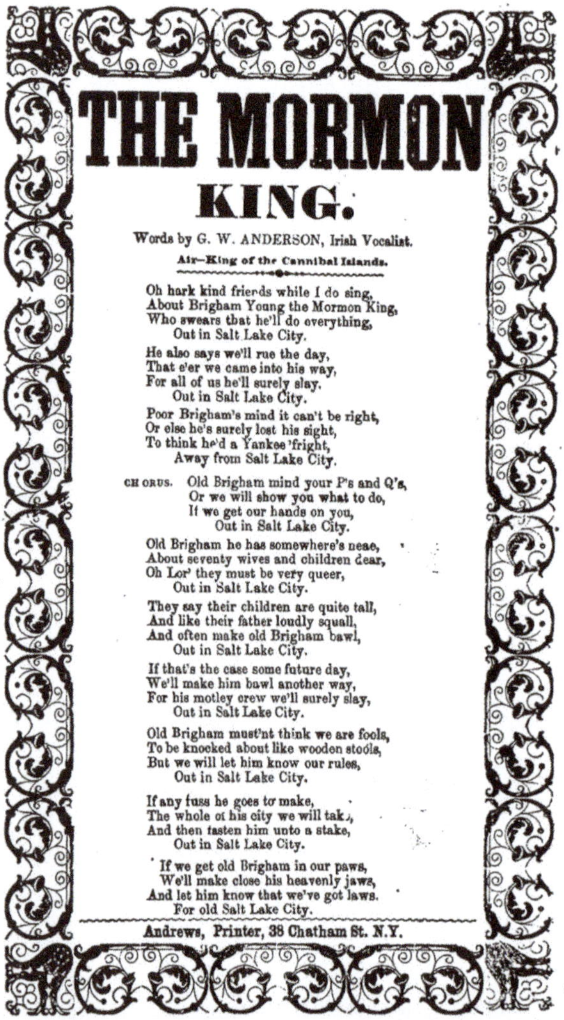

THE MORMON KING.

Words by G. W. ANDERSON, Irish Vocalist.

Air—King of the Cannibal Islands.

Oh hark kind friends while I do sing,
About Brigham Young the Mormon King,
Who swears that he'll do everything,
Out in Salt Lake City.

He also says we'll rue the day,
That e'er we came into his way,
For all of us he'll surely slay.
Out in Salt Lake City.

Poor Brigham's mind it can't be right,
Or else he's surely lost his sight,
To think he'd a Yankee 'fright,
Away from Salt Lake City.

CHORUS. Old Brigham mind your P's and Q's,
Or we will show you what to do,
If we get our hands on you,
Out in Salt Lake City.

Old Brigham he has somewhere's neae,
About seventy wives and children dear,
Oh Lor' they must be very queer,
Out in Salt Lake City.

They say their children are quite tall,
And like their father loudly squall,
And often make old Brigham bawl,
Out in Salt Lake City.

If that's the case some future day,
We'll make him bawl another way,
For his motley crew we'll surely slay,
Out in Salt Lake City.

Old Brigham must'nt think we are fools,
To be knocked about like wooden stools,
But we will let him know our rules,
Out in Salt Lake City.

If any fuss he goes to make,
The whole of his city we will take,
And then fasten him unto a stake,
Out in Salt Lake City.

If we get old Brigham in our paws,
We'll make close his heavenly jaws,
And let him know that we've got laws.
For old Salt Lake City.

Andrews, Printer, 38 Chatham St. N.Y.

As suggested by these 1860 song lyrics by G. W. Anderson, many Americans were hostile toward the Mormons.

Omaha, Nebraska. The railroad had conquered the Great American Desert. Nearly bankrupt and facing a desperate labor shortage, they began the last leg of the race.

The Mormon settlement in Salt Lake City, Utah, was in many ways self-sufficient. Before the arrival of the railroad, it was the only white settlement along the Platte Valley route between the Sierra Nevada and Omaha, Nebraska. The Mormons were primarily farmers until the spring of 1868. That year, thick swarms of grasshoppers had descended on the fields of central Utah, destroying the crops and, with them, the economy. Farmers were forced to abandon their fields, leaving thousands of young men in need of work.

The Mormons proved to be skilled and reliable railroad workers. They

TWO LEADERS TALK

On May 6, 1868, Thomas Durant sent an urgent telegram to Brigham Young, the leader of the Mormon Church. Durant asked Young to assemble a crew of laborers to make the grade from Echo Canyon, Utah, to the Great Salt Lake, and to name his price. Young had an interest in the completion of the railroad and was eager to have the two tracks meet in Salt Lake City. He believed the railroad would bring manufactured goods, religious converts, and tourists. He instantly agreed. While the Union Pacific tracklayers were approaching the Utah border from the east, the Mormons went to work leveling a grade for about $2 per day each.

carved the frozen ground during the day and cleared the rubble by the light of brushfires at night. Unlike the hell-on-wheels towns, the Mormon camp was quiet and safe. The Mormons didn't drink, gamble, or engage in violent behavior, and the Union Pacific officials agreed that they were ideal employees. Durant, however, refused to pay them. Instead, he had paid the Union Pacific stockholders, himself included, 300-percent dividends on their investment that year,and therefore did not have the money to pay more than half of the Mormon workforce. Durant was running the Union Pacific into the ground, and the board of directors was eager to get rid of him.

★ CHAPTER FIVE

THE TRACKS MEET

The place where the two railroads would meet at last was set at Promontory Summit, Utah. It is 37 miles (59 km) north of Promontory Point, and it looks down on the northern end of the Great Salt Lake. The historic event attracted crowds. Four companies of soldiers and a band joined them. Cast just for the event, a golden spike was presented to the railroads by a San Francisco contractor. The solid gold spike would be placed at the meeting of the tracks and tapped into place by Central Pacific president Leland Stanford. At noon on May 10, 1869, a telegraph wire connected to the spike transmitted the sound of Stanford driving home the ceremonial spike across the country.

THE END OF THE EFFORT

Two trains, the Central Pacific's Jupiter and the Union Pacific's Number 119, faced each other on the tracks. After several speeches, the final wooden tie, made of laurel, was brought forward and put in place. Thomas Durant gave one tap on

Thomas Hill's circa 1881 painting *The Last Spike* included two Chinese laborers on the track and a Native American at the right of the crowd. Both represent the nameless people who died during construction.

the last spike, and Stanford prepared to finish the job. Stanford swung his hammer and missed, instead striking the iron rail. Indistinguishable from the real thing over the telegraph wire, it was announced that the spike had been hammered into place and the telegraph report was subsequently cut. Bells were rung around the country, and everyone began to celebrate. The Jupiter and the Number 119 moved toward each other until their noses nearly touched. Then both trains separated, and each was ceremoniously pulled over the final rail in turn. The job was done.

The words "The Last Spike" are carved on the head of the golden spike: "The Pacific Railroad, ground broken Jany 8th 1863; completed May 8th 1869," referring to the original date planned for the final ceremony. Another side reads "May God continue for the unity of our Country as the Railroad unites the two great Oceans of the world." Carved in the remaining two sides are all the names of the officers of the Central Pacific and Union Pacific railroad companies.

For the Big Four, Durant, Dodge, all their investors and employees, and all of the Americans who eagerly followed the story as it unfolded in their local newspapers, the saga of the transcontinental railroad was not yet over. Durant still had not paid Brigham Young for the grade between Echo Canyon and the Great Salt Lake, a job that had begun nearly a year before. With the Union Pacific virtually bankrupt, Durant was forced to pay Young in nearly $600,000 worth of railroad equipment. Young was eager to get into the railroad business himself, and the Mormons quickly built a successful spur between Ogden, Utah, and Salt Lake City. Only weeks after the golden spike was hammered in, Durant was voted off the Union Pacific's board of directors, and he left the railroad business for good.

In 1872, the *New York Sun* broke the story of the Crédit Mobilier and corruption within the railroad companies. The United States House of Representatives investigated allegations against Crédit Mobilier and the Central Pacific and Union Pacific railroads. It became clear that the men who ran the railroads had profited immensely from the enterprise by bribing and cheating the government, exploiting their labor force, and ignoring debts they incurred along the way. Perhaps not accidentally, however, the Central Pacific's records had been lost in a fire. The Union Pacific, despite overwhelming proof of its corruption, was given only an official censure from the House of Representatives. America's first national corporations had escaped investigation essentially unharmed. Dodge and the Big Four worked for the railroads for the rest of their lives, and their names became legendary in the business.

HISTORIC STAMPS

Before 1869, every stamp issued by the United States Post Office displayed a portrait of George Washington, Benjamin Franklin, Thomas Jefferson, Andrew Jackson, or Abraham Lincoln—the elder statesmen of the American nation. In 1869, the Post Office broke the mold. Two three-cent stamps were issued that illustrated a new era of American patriotism. One shows a Pony Express rider on horseback, celebrating the overland mail service that was by then out of business. The other stamp shows a gleaming, wood-burning railroad engine. Smoke billows from its smokestack as it chugs across an open field. The train was the new symbol of American freedom.

RIDING THE RAILS

Once the last rail was laid, passengers could travel from New York to San Francisco in seven days. There were three classes of cars: first, second, and third, or emigrant, class. As the railroad expanded, the price decreased, making the journey even more accessible to everyone. In 1870, passengers paid $136 (the equivalent of about $1,477 today) for first-class passage across the country. They rode, slept, and dined in elegant Pullman cars outfitted with the comforts of home. That same year, $110 (roughly $1,194 today) would buy a second-class ticket across the country, and for just $65 (about $705 today) a traveler could go by emigrant car.

Trains were sometimes caught in winter storms in the Sierra Nevada and were forced to wait out the bad weather at the nearest station town. With decreasing frequency, the cars were attacked by Native Americans, most of whom had either been killed or moved to reservations. Still, the railroad was the safest and fastest way to travel long distances, and in the days before highways and automobiles, the romance of the open rail captivated the American imagination.

Throughout the construction of the railroad, local newspapers chronicled its every step. Stories of Indian attacks frightened readers, tales of corruption and scandal shocked them, and details of the project's unprecedented progress roused their patriotism. The country was gripped by, as one railroad official described it, "railroadmania." Proof of this came in the unlikely form of new postage stamps.

It may be difficult to appreciate the courage and genius required to build a railroad stretching 1,774 miles (2,855 km) through uncharted wilderness. Theodore Judah,

The travelers in this drawing from 1872 ride in luxury in a Pullman palace car on the Pacific Railroad. Third-class passengers sat in other cars on stiff wooden benches.

Grenville Dodge, the Big Four, and Thomas Durant led an army of twenty thousand men into the wilderness and changed America forever. The transcontinental railroad ushered in a new era of communication, social progress, and cultural diversity, as ideas and products traveled as quickly as a telegraph signal or a speeding train. It did so at an exceptionally high price, however, for this new era dawned at the expense of the immigrant laborers who had worked the rails and the Indians who had fought against the railroad revolution. In the end, like many great human accomplishments, the building of a transcontinental railroad signaled the beginning of one era and the end of another. It was an unprecedented act of creation and a force of horrible destruction. We can only marvel at its construction and wonder what the world might be like had it never been done.

TIMELINE

1848 Gold is discovered west of Sacramento, California.

1853 Congress sponsors surveyors to suggest possible routes for a transcontinental railroad west of the Mississippi.

1856 General Grenville Dodge chooses the Platte Valley route for a transcontinental railroad.

1861 Abraham Lincoln becomes president; the thirteen states of the Confederacy secede from the Union, and the American Civil War begins.

June 28, 1861 The Central Pacific Railroad Company is organized, with Leland Stanford as president.

1862 The Homestead Act is ratified by Congress.

July 1, 1862 President Lincoln signs the Pacific Railroad Act, which creates the Union Pacific Railroad Company under the authority of a board of directors chosen by Congress.

January 8, 1863 The Central Pacific breaks ground on Front and K Streets in Sacramento, California.

November 2, 1863 Theodore Judah, the chief engineer of the Union Pacific Railroad Company, dies in New York after having contracted yellow fever in Panama.

April 1865 President Lincoln is assassinated; two weeks later, the South surrenders, ending the Civil War.

November 30, 1867 The first Central Pacific train rides the rails through the Summit Tunnel, the longest and most elevated tunnel on the Central Pacific line.

January 9, 1869 The Union Pacific lays its 1,000th mile of track west of Omaha, Nebraska.

May 10, 1869 The last spike is hammered into the rails, joining the Union Pacific and Central Pacific Railroads in Promontory Summit, Utah.

NATIONAL REPUBLICAN PLATFORM ADOPTED BY THE NATIONAL REPUBLICAN CONVENTION, HELD IN CHICAGO, MAY 17, 1860

Resolved, That we the delegated representatives of the Republican electors of the United States, in Convention assembled, in discharge of the duty we owe to our constituents and our country, unite in the following declarations:

The Republican Party.

1. That the history of the nation during the last four years, has fully established the propriety and necessity of the organization and perpetuation of the Republican party, and that the causes which called it in [omitted word] existence are permanent in their nature, and now, more than ever before, demand its peaceful and constitutional triumph.

Its Fundamental Principles.

2. That the maintenance of the principles promulgated in the Declaration of Independence and embodied in the Federal Constitution, "That all men are created equal; that they are endowed by their Creator with certain inalienable rights that among these are life, liberty and the [omitted, two words] that to secure these rights, governments are instituted [omitted, two words] deriving their just powers [omitted word] the preservation [omitted word] and shall be preserved.

[Omitted word] Union.

3. That to the [omitted word] the States, this nation owes its unprecedented increase of population, its surprising development of material resources, its rapid augmentation of wealth, its happiness at home and its honor abroad and we hold in abhorrence all schemes for Disunion, come from whatever source they may: And we congratulate the country that the Republican member of Congress has uttered or countenanced the threats

of Disunion so often made by the Democratic member without [omitted word] and with applause from their political associates; and we [omitted word] those threats of Disunion, in case of a popular overthrow of their ascendancy as denying the vital principles of a free government, as an avowal of contemplated treason, which it is the imperative duty of an indignant People sternly to rebuke and forever silence.

State Sovereignty.

4. That the maintenance inviolate of the Rights of the States, and especially the right of each State to order and control its own domestic institutions according to its own judgment exclusively, is essential to that balance of power on which the perfection and endurance of our political fabric depends; and we denounce the lawless invasion by armed force of the soil of any State or Territory, no matter under what pretext, as among the gravest of crimes.

Sectionalism and Democracy.

5. That the present Democratic Administration has far exceeded our worst apprehensions, in its measureless subserviency to the [omitted word] of a sectional interest, as especially evinced in its desperate exertions to force the infamous Lecompton Constitution upon the protesting people of Kansas; in construing the personal relation between master and servant to involve an unqualified property in persons; in its attempted enforcement, everywhere, on land and sea, through the intervention of Congress and of the Federal Courts, of the extreme pretensions of a purely local interest; and in its general and unvarying abuse of power entrusted to it by a confiding people.

Its Extravagance and Corruption.

6. That the people justly view with alarm the reckless extravagance which pervades every department of the Federal Government; that a return to rigid economy and

accountability is indispensable to arrest the systematic plunder of the public treasury by favored partisans; while the recent startling developments of frauds and corruptions at the Federal metropolis, show that an entire change of administration is imperatively demanded.

A Dangerous Political Heresy.

7. That the new dogma that the Constitution, of its own force, carries Slavery into any or all of the Territories of the United States, is a dangerous political heresy, at variance with the explicit provisions of that instrument itself, with contemporaneous exposition, and with legislative and judicial precedent; is revolutionary in its tendency, and subversive of the peace and harmony of the country.

Freedom, the Normal Condition of Territories.

8. That the normal condition of all the territory of the United States is that of Freedom: That as our Republican fathers, when they had abolished slavery in all our national territory, ordained that "no person should be deprived of life, liberty, or property, without due process of law," it becomes our duty, by legislation, whenever such legislation is necessary, to maintain this provision of the Constitution, against all attempts to violate it; and we deny the authority of Congress, of a territorial legislature, or of any individuals, to give legal existence to slavery in any Territory of the United States.

The African Slave Trade.

9. That we brand the recent re-opening of the African Slave Trade, under the cover of our national flag, aided by perversions of judicial power, as a crime against humanity and a burning shame to our country and age; and we call upon Congress to take prompt and efficient measures for the total and final suppression of that execrable traffic.

Democratic Popular Sovereignty.

10. [Omitted word] the recent vetoes, by their Federal Government of the sets of the Legislatures of Kansas and Nebraska, prohibiting Slavery in those Territories, we find a practical illustration of the boasted Democratic principle of Non-Intervention and Popular Sovereignty embodied in the Kansas-Nebraska Bill and a demonstration of the deception and fraud involved therein.

Admission of Kansas.

11. That Kansas should, of right, be immediately admitted as a [omitted word] under the Constitution recently formed and adopted by her people, and accepted by the House of Representatives.

Encouragement of American Industry.

12. That, while providing revenue for the support of the general government by duties upon her imports, sound policy requires such an adjustment of these imports as to encourage the development of the industrial interests of the whole country; and we commend that policy or national exchanges, which secures to the working men liberal wages, to agriculture remunerating prices, to mechanics and manufacturers an adequate reward for their skill, labor, and enterprise, and to the nation commercial prosperity and independence.

Free Homesteads.

13. That we protest against any sale or alienation to others of the Public Lands held by actual settlers, and against any view of the Free Homestead policy which regards the settlers as paupers or suppliants for public bounty; and we demand the passage by Congress of the complete and satisfactory Homestead Measure which has already passed the House.

Rights of Citizenship.

14. That the Republican party is opposed to any [omitted word] in our Naturalization Laws or any State Legislation by which [omitted, two words] of citizenship hitherto accorded to [omitted word] from [omitted word] shall be abridged or impaired, and in favor of giving a full and [omitted word] protection to the rights of all classes of [omitted, three words] whether native or naturalized, both at home and abroad.

River and Harbor Improvements.

15. The appropriations by Congress for River and Harbor Improvements of a National character, required for the accommodation and security of an existing commerce, are authorized by the Constitution, and justified by the obligation of Government to protect the lives and property of its citizens.

A Pacific Railroad.

16. That a Railroad to the Pacific Ocean is imperatively demanded by the interests of the whole country that the Federal Government ought to render immediate and efficient aid in its construction; and that, as preliminary thereto, a daily overland Mail should be promptly established.

Co-operation Invited.

17. Finally, having thus set forth our distinctive principles and views, we invite the co-operations of all citizens, however differing on other questions, who substantially agree with us in their affirmance and support.

PACIFIC RAILWAY ACT (1862)
PARTIAL TRANSCRIPTION

CHAP. CXX. — An Act to aid in the Construction of a Railroad and Telegraph Line from the Missouri River to the Pacific Ocean, and to secure to the Government the Use of the same for Postal, Military, and Other Purposes.

Be it enacted by the Senate and House of Representatives of the United States of America in Congress assembled, That [numerous individuals] .... together with commissioners to be appointed by the Secretary of the Interior, and all persons who shall or may be associated with them, and their successors, are hereby created and erected into a body corporate and politic in deed and in law, by the name, style, and title of "The Union Pacific Railroad Company; " and by that name shall have perpetual succession, and shall be able to sue and to be sued, plead and be impleaded, defend and be defended, in all courts of law and equity within the United States, and may make and have a common seal; and the said corporation is hereby authorized and empowered to layout, locate, construct, furnish, maintain, and enjoy a continuous railroad and telegraph, with the appurtenances, from a point on the one hundredth meridian of longitude west from Greenwich, between the south margin of the valley of the Republican River and the north margin of the valley of the Platte River, in the Territory of Nebraska, to the western boundary of Nevada Territory, upon the route and terms hereinafter provided, and is hereby vested with all the powers, privileges, and immunities necessary to carry into effect the purposes of this act as herein set forth.

GLOSSARY

alkali Salty; related to soil composition.

ballast A heavy material used to secure stability for an object or construction.

black powder A chemical explosive made of potassium nitrate, charcoal, and sulfur.

bond A document issued by a government or company that promised a payment at a time in the future.

collateral A security on a loan that is offered by the borrower to protect the lender's investment.

dividends Shares of profit.

grade The level land on which the ties and rails are laid.

laurel A kind of evergreen tree.

lode A deposit of a mineral.

mogul A great figure in business.

nitroglycerin A chemical explosive, more volatile than black powder.

platforms Written declarations of an individual's or political party's principles and beliefs.

roadbed The flat surface on which the ties, rails, and ballast of a railroad track are laid.

schooner A large, two-masted sailboat.

spur A railroad track that branches off from the main track.

summit The highest point.

surveyor A person who determines the contour of land using mathematical calculations.

ties Long pieces of wood that railroad rails are spiked into.

B&O Railroad Museum
901 West Pratt Street
Baltimore, MD 21223
(410) 752-2490
Email: info@borail.org
Website: http://www.borail.org
Facebook: @BandORailroadMuseum
Twitter: @borrm
Instagram: @borailroad
This museum holds the oldest and most complete collection of railroad history and includes nineteenth- and twentieth-century railroad equipment, original standing shop buildings, and tracks.

California State Railroad Museum
125 I Street
Sacramento, CA 95814
(916) 323-9280
Website: https://www.californiarailroad.museum
Facebook: @CaliforniaStateRailroadMuseumFoundation
Twitter and Instagram: @csrm_foundation
The museum complex displays twenty-one restored locomotives, a Pullman-style sleeping car, and a dining car filled with railroad china to tell the story of railroad history in California and the West.

Canadian Museum of History
100 Laurier Street
Gatineau, Quebec K1A 0M8
Canada
(800) 555-5621
Website: http://www.historymuseum.ca
Facebook, Twitter, and Instagram: @CanMusHistory

This museum features multiple exhibits on the colonization of Canada and the transportation changes the country underwent.

Canadian War Museum
1 Vimy Place
Ottawa, Ontario K1A 0M8
Canada
(800) 555-5621
Website: http://www.warmuseum.ca
Facebook, Twitter, and Instagram: @CanMusHistory
Canada's involvement in armed conflicts are featured in this 25,000 square meter (269,000 square foot) facility visited by 1.2 million people each year.

Golden Spike National Historic Site
Mailing Address:
PO Box 897
Brigham City, UT 84302
(435) 471-2209 x29
Physical Address:
6200 North 22300 West
Promontory Summit, UT 84307
Website: https://www.nps.gov/gosp/index.htm
The park includes a visitors center, a replica of the Central Pacific and Union Pacific railroad track meeting point, and replica steam locomotives.

Nevada State Railroad Museum, Carson City
2180 S. Carson Street
Carson City, NV 89701
(775) 687.6953
Facebook: @NSRMCC

Twitter: @NVMuseums
Website: http://nvculture.org
/nevadastaterailroadmuseumcarsoncity
This museum includes locomotives and cars from the Virginia & Truckee Railroad and other railroads in Nevada.

Union Pacific Railroad Museum
200 Pearl Street
Council Bluffs, Iowa 51503
(712) 329-8307
Website: http://www.uprrmuseum.org
Facebook and Twitter: @uprrmuseum
This museum includes artifacts, documents, photographs, and equipment from the construction of the transcontinental railroad.

FOR FURTHER READING

Behnke, Alison. *A Timeline History of the Transcontinental Railroad*. Minneapolis, MN: Lerner Publications, 2016.

Caravantes, Peggy. *The Building of the Transcontinental Railroad*. Mankato, MN: The Child's World, 2017.

Gibson, Karen Bush. *Oregon Trail: The Journey Across the Country from Lewis and Clark to the Transcontinental Railroad*. White River Junction, VT: Nomad Press, 2017.

Linde, Barbara M. *Native Americans in Early North America*. New York, NY: Lucent Press, 2017.

Mason Crest. *North America*. Broomall, PA: Mason Crest, 2016.

Otfinoski, Steven. *The Building of the Transcontinental Railroad: An Interactive Engineering Adventure*. North Mankato, MN: Capstone Press, 2015.

Rajczak, Michael. *The Transcontinental Railroad*. New York, NY: Gareth Stevens Library, 2014.

Shea, Therese. *Cornelius Vanderbilt and the Railroad Industry*. New York, NY: Rosen Publishing, 2017.

Uhl, Xina M. *The Railroad, the Telegraph, and Other Technologies*. New York, NY: Britannica Educational Publishing, 2018.

Wolfe, James. *The Industrial Revolution: Steam and Steel*. New York, NY: Britannica Educational Publishing, 2016.

BIBLIOGRAPHY

Ambrose, Stephen. *Nothing Like It in the World: The Men Who Built the Transcontinental Railroad.* New York, NY: Simon and Schuster, 2000.

Beebe, Lucius. *The Central Pacific and the Southern Pacific Railroads*. Berkeley, CA: Howell-North, 1963.

Chinn, Thomas W., H. Mark Lai, and Philip P. Choy, eds. *A History of the Chinese in California*. San Francisco, CA: The Chinese Historical Society of America, 1969.

Howard, Robert West. *The Great Iron Trail: The Story of the First Transcontinental Railroad.* New York, NY: GP Putnam's Sons, 1962.

Huffman, Wendell W. "Iron Horse Along the Truckee: The Central Pacific Reaches Nevada." *Nevada State Historical Society Quarterly*, Vol. 38, No. 1, Spring 1995, pp. 19–36.

Huffman, Wendell W. "Railroads Shipped by Sea." *Railroad History*, Bulletin 180, Spring 1999, pp. 7–30.

Kraus, George. "Chinese Laborers and the Construction of the Central Pacific." *Utah Historical Quarterly*, Vol. 37, No. 1, Winter 1969, pp. 41–57.

McCague, James. *Moguls and Iron Men: The Story of the First Transcontinental Railroad*. New York, NY: Harper and Row, 1964.

PBS.org. "Primary Sources." Retrieved on March 30, 2018. http://www.pbs.org/kera/usmexicanwar/resources/manifest_destiny_sullivan.html.

Steiner, Stan. *Fusang: The Chinese Who Built America.* New York, NY: Harper and Row, 1979.

United States Senate. "Landmark Legislation: The Pacific Railway Act of 1862." Retrieved on March 29, 2018. https://www.senate.gov/artandhistory/history/common/generic/PacificRailwayActof1862.htm.

Warman, Cy. *The Story of the Railroad*. New York, NY: D. Appleton and Company, 1998.

INDEX

ABOUT THE AUTHORS

Xina M. Uhl discovered her love of history while still in grade school. She went on to obtain a master of arts in history from California State University, Northridge. After teaching college-level American history, she moved into educational writing. She has authored numerous nonfiction books for young people. When she is not writing or reading, she enjoys travel, photography, and hiking with her dogs. Her blog features book reviews, her travel adventures, and her latest fiction projects.

Gillian Houghton is an editor and writer living in New York City. Her most recent railroad trip took her from New York's Pennsylvania Station to her hometown of Milwaukee, Wisconsin. She plans to traverse the western half of the country by rail soon.

PHOTO CREDITS

Cover Ed Vebell/Archive Photos/Getty Images; cover, p. 1 (flag) Piotr Krzeslak/Shutterstock.com; cover, p. 1 (scroll) Aleksandrs Bondars/Shutterstock.com; p. 3 Lone Wolf Photography /Shutterstock.com; pp. 4–5 (background) Enigmangels /Shutterstock.com; pp. 5 (inset) Library of Congress Geography and Map Division; pp. 7, 16, 25, 34, 42 (background) Peter Gudella/Shutterstock.com; p. 9 Print Collector/Hulton Archive /Getty Images; pp. 10, 21, 38 Library of Congress Prints and Photographs Division; pp. 14, 17, 40 Library of Congress Rare Book And Special Collections Division; p. 19 Everett Historical /Shutterstock.com; p. 25 (inset) National Archives and Records Administration; pp. 28, 34 Bettmann/Getty Images; p. 30 Private Collection/Tarker/Bridgeman Images; p. 32 Union Pacific Railroad Museum; p. 36 Pictures from History/Bridgeman Images; p. 43 GraphicaArtis/Archive Photos/Getty Images; p. 47 Three Lions /Hulton Archive/Getty Images.

Design: Michael Moy; Layout: Nicole Russo-Duca; Photo Researcher: Nicole DiMella